THANKFUL FOR JESUS

HEATHER HART

The author of this book can be contacted for permissions, additional copies, and speaking inquiries at the following address:

Heather Hart
P.O. Box 1277
Seymour, TX 76380

CONTENTS

I AM THANKFUL...

INTRODUCTION:

THANKFUL FOR JESUS

When was the last time we were simply thankful for Jesus?

When we count our blessings, we usually thank God for the things He has created or put in our lives, such as our family and friends, a roof over our heads, and food in our bellies. Don't get me wrong, all of these are great blessings that come from God, but when was the last time you were simply thankful for Jesus, not just who He is, but what He means in our lives?

That's what you'll find in this book. Thirty devotions that are all about Jesus to help you cultivate some gospel gratitude.

1

JESUS CREATED EVERYTHING

For by him all things were created,
in heaven and on earth, visible and invisible, whether
thrones or dominions or rulers or authorities—all things
were created through him and for him.

Colossians 1:16

In my Bible next to the opening verses of Genesis, I wrote a note that says, "Faith starts here." It's a reminder from Hebrews 11:3, "By faith we understand that the universe was created by the word of God, so that what is seen was not made out of things that are visible."

Before the earth came into being, there was Jesus. Genesis says that God hovered over the formless void and then He spoke the earth into existence. Every mountain and every valley were created by Jesus. Colossians 1:16 says that, "For by him all things were created."

Every ant on the ground and cloud in the sky, they all exist because of Jesus. Every sunset and every raindrop are the work of His hand. As Psalm 19:1 says, "The heavens declare the glory of God, and the sky above proclaims his handiwork. Jesus is the Word of God (John 1:1), and He created it all.

Today, that truth leaves me thankful for all of creation.

PRAYER OF GOSPEL GRATITUDE

Father God, thank You for creating the world. Please help me remember that it's all the work of Your hands as I go about my day. You are the master craftsman, and I am so thankful to know You. In the name of Your Son, Jesus, I pray, amen.

2

THERE IS NO CONDEMNATION

There is therefore now no condemnation
for those who are in Christ Jesus.

Romans 8:1

Romans 3:23 tells us that we have all sinned and fallen short of the glory of God. Which means we all deserve God's wrath, both as a whole and for all the little things we get wrong every day. But that's not the way of our God.

Romans 8:1 is one of my favorite Bible verses. It tells us that "There is therefore now no condemnation for those who are in Christ Jesus." None.

It doesn't matter what you've done in the past, what you're struggling with today, or what you'll do tomorrow. All of your sins are covered by the blood of Christ. If you belong to Jesus, you stand forgiven and free, both now and always.

That time you broke the rules in high school: Forgiven.

That time you lied to your boss: Forgiven.

The sins that are so big you don't even want to think about them: Forgiven.

And if God has forgiven you, don't you think it's time to forgive yourself?

Romans 5:8 says, "But God shows his love for us in that while we were still sinners, Christ died for us." That's good news. And today, it leaves me thankful that there is no condemnation for those who belong to Jesus.

PRAYER OF GOSPEL GRATITUDE

Father God, thank You for loving me even when I didn't deserve it. Sometimes I still don't feel worthy of Your love, but I know You love me, anyway. Thank You for that. Help me rest in the forgiveness You offer. In the name of Your Son, who died on the cross for me; amen.

3

JESUS CARES FOR US

Cast all your anxiety on him because he cares for you.

1 Peter 5:7 NIV

I love that we are loved by God. Everyone worries sometimes. Today's verse reminds us of the truth that we can turn to Jesus when we get stressed out or anxious. We can always come to Him because He cares for us.

Jesus loved us so much that He humbled Himself to be killed on a cross. In everything He did on earth, He showed His great love for us. When we are stressed out and having a bad day, Jesus cares. "For we do not have a high priest who is unable to sympathize with our weaknesses, but one who in every respect has been tempted as we are, yet without sin" (Hebrews 4:15). Jesus doesn't just care, He gets it. He's been in our shoes, and He had bad days.

Sure, culture was different back when He walked the earth, but He did walk the earth. And Jesus told us in the book of John, "Greater love has no one than this, that someone lay down his life for his friends" (v. 15:13). That's how much Jesus cares for us.

In Matthew 10:30-31, Jesus promised that we are worth more to Him than the sparrows, and that He has the hairs on our head numbered. If He cares about something as trivial as that, then we can trust He cares about what concerns us—big or small. That's why I'm thankful for Jesus today.

PRAYER OF GOSPEL GRATITUDE

Father God, You love me and care about me so much. You are omnipotent, God of all, and yet You care about me and my life. Jesus was (and is) the perfect picture of Your love for me. Help me to cast all my cares on You, because I know You care.

4

JESUS IS GOD WITH US

Have I not commanded you? Be strong and courageous. Do not be frightened, and do not be dismayed, for the LORD your God is with you wherever you go.

Joshua 1:9

Jesus is Immanuel: God with us. And He is with us—every moment of every day.

Psalm 139:7-10 says, "Where shall I go from your Spirit? Or where shall I flee from your presence? If I ascend to heaven, you are there! If I make my bed in Sheol, you are there! If I take the wings of the morning and dwell in the uttermost parts of the sea, even there your hand shall lead me, and your right hand shall hold me."

No matter what you're facing today, you can do so knowing that God is with you. I don't know how today will work itself out, but God does. He knows the end from the beginning, and He will be with you every step of the way. No matter what you're going through or how far from God you feel, He is never more than a prayer away.

PRAYER OF GOSPEL GRATITUDE

Father God, thank You for always being with me... that I don't have to face this world alone. Thank You for being Immanuel.

5

JESUS IS NEAR TO THE BROKENHEARTED

He heals the brokenhearted
and binds up their wounds.

Psalm 147:3

Nestled in the book of Genesis, we find the story of Hagar. She was a slave woman who was mistreated by her mistress and then sent away with her young son. She was exiled, weary, and alone, but God saw her. She lifted her voice and wept, (Genesis 21:16) and God heard her.

Hagar's story is a beautiful reminder that we don't have a God who is far away, but a God who is near to the brokenhearted (Psalm 34:18). When our heart hurts, we can take it to Jesus. First Peter 5:7 tells us to cast our anxiety on Christ, because He cares for us.

In the book of Matthew, Jesus said that God clothes the lilies of the field, and He cares for the birds of the air, even though they are here today and gone tomorrow, so just imagine how much more He cares for us, the people created in His image.

Romans 8:26 says, "Likewise the Spirit helps us in our weakness. For we do not know what to pray for as we ought, but the Spirit Himself intercedes for us with groanings too deep for words." When our heart hurts so badly, we don't even know what to pray, God still hears us. Today, I'm thankful that Jesus is near to us even when our hearts are breaking.

PRAYER OF GOSPEL GRATITUDE

Father God, thank You for being near to the brokenhearted, for hearing the groanings of my heart when I can't find the words to pray. Thank You for loving me and always providing for me. In Jesus' name I pray, amen.

6

THE BLOOD OF CHRIST

For this is my blood of the covenant, which is poured out
for many for the forgiveness of sins.

Matthew 26:28

God loves us so much He sent Jesus to die on a cross as punishment for our sins—yours and mine. But did you know that death on a cross was so much more than execution? It was reserved for the worst criminal as the ultimate punishment. Crucifixion was a horrific, prolonged torture leading only to death. That's what Jesus endured for us.

When we say our sins are covered by the blood of Jesus, it's blood that was poured out on the cross. Every drop was wrought with pain, but Jesus hung there because of His great love for us.

The apostle Paul said it this way in his letter to the Ephesians, "In him we have redemption through his blood, the forgiveness of our trespasses, according to the riches of his grace" (Ephesians 1:7). And then it goes on to say, "But now in Christ Jesus you who once were far off have been brought near by the blood of Christ" (Ephesians 2:13).

The blood of Jesus made a way for us to be forgiven for our sins. Jesus took our punishment on Himself so we could have an eternity to spend with the One who created us.

In the words of Isaiah, "He was pierced for our transgressions; he was crushed for our iniquities; upon him was the chastisement that brought us peace, and with his wounds we are healed" (v. 53:5). And I am so thankful for the blood of Christ.

PRAYER OF GOSPEL GRATITUDE

Father God, thank You for sending Jesus to die for my sins. Thank You for the love You poured out on the cross and for the pain You endured. Thank You, Lord, for all of it.

7

THE LOVE OF JESUS IS UNENDING

For I am sure that neither death nor life,
nor angels nor rulers, nor things present nor things to come,
nor powers, nor height nor depth, nor anything else in all
creation, will be able to separate us from the love of God in
Christ Jesus our Lord.

Romans 8:38-39

First John 4:8 tells us that God is love. We have a God who doesn't just love us when we do good, but a God who is love at the very core of His being. That means He loves at all times—the good, the bad, and the in-between.

That said, I love the reminder found in Romans 8 that nothing can separate us from God's love. God loves us. Period. It doesn't matter what we have done in the past, or the mistakes we will make today. He just loves us unconditionally. He can't help it, because it's who He is. He overflows with love for us, especially when we don't deserve it. Romans 5:8 says, "God shows his love for us in that while we were still sinners, Christ died for us." That's the God we have.

I don't know about you, but I'm far from perfect. I struggle on a daily basis. That's why today I'm thankful that God's love is unending.

PRAYER OF GOSPEL GRATITUDE

Father God, thank You for loving me. I'm so thankful that You don't just kind of like me, but that You love me with all of You because You are love.

8

JESUS KNOWS THE
END FROM THE BEGINNING

I am the Alpha and the Omega, the first and the last,
the beginning and the end.

Revelation 22:13

Corrie Ten Boom once said, "When a train goes through a tunnel and it gets dark, you don't throw away the ticket and jump off. You sit still and trust the engineer." And so it is with our Christian life.

When life gets tough, we shouldn't toss our relationship with Jesus out the window. We should dig into Him and let Him be our refuge, because He already knows how our struggle will end. He sees the end from the beginning, and we can trust Him with our future.

I don't know about you, but I take a great deal of comfort in the fact that God knows the end from the beginning. It helps me to trust Him instead of worrying about what will come next. I can trust that whatever it is, God is already there. He knows what will happen. He will be with me every step of the way, and He's got this (whatever "this" is).

PRAYER OF GOSPEL GRATITUDE

Father God, I am so thankful that You know the end from the beginning. I love that I can trust You no matter what comes next.

9

EVERY DAY IS A NEW DAY WITH JESUS

The steadfast love of the LORD never ceases;
his mercies never come to an end;
they are new every morning;
great is your faithfulness.

Lamentations 3:22-23

I love that God's love and mercy are new every morning. It doesn't matter what happened yesterday, we will never out-sin the work Jesus did on the cross. We will never out-sin the love and mercy of our God. His love is steadfast and sure. It never ceases.

Sometimes I get stuck in the past, like the time I messed up in high school and did the wrong thing. The time lied to my boss haunts me because I knew better. However, I can counter those thoughts, and any others, by remembering that there is no condemnation for those who belong to Jesus (Romans 8:1). I can live with a clear conscience because God has already forgiven me.

Yet, when I do struggle with those thoughts, God's love and mercy are new. He forgave me for my sins years ago, and He isn't holding them against me now. He gives me the grace I need to forgive myself and keep putting one foot in front of the other.

PRAYER OF GOSPEL GRATITUDE

Father God, thank You so much that Your love and mercy are new every morning. Thank You that I can put my trust in You, even when the things of this world weigh me down.

10

JESUS GIVES US REST

Come to me, all who labor and are heavy laden, and I will give you rest. Take my yoke upon you, and learn from me, for I am gentle and lowly in heart, and you will find rest for your souls. For my yoke is easy, and my burden is light.

Matthew 11:28-30

Have you ever been so overwhelmed by life that you didn't know what to do next? I have. It's not a fun place to be in, but in today's world, it happens all too often. That's why I love these verses in Matthew.

Jesus calls us to come to Him when we're weary, and He will give us rest by taking the burden off our shoulders. Instead of worrying about everything going on, we can place it at His feet and trust that He will work it all out.

Sometimes that's easier said than done, am I right?

Sometimes we place something at the feet of Jesus and then pick it right back up again. It can be hard to surrender control (or even the elusion of control). But that's what Jesus calls us to do. That's the yoke He wants us to take on—to learn from Him and trust Him no matter what comes our way. And when we learn to trust in Jesus, then He will give us rest for our soul.

PRAYER OF GOSPEL GRATITUDE

Father God, thank You for sending Jesus. Thank You that He is capable of taking all our sins and sorrows upon Himself. Please help me to lay my troubles at His feet and trust in Him alone.

11

JESUS IS OUR REFUGE

This God—his way is perfect;
the word of the LORD proves true;
he is a shield for all those who take
refuge in him.

Psalm 18:30

When was the last time you took refuge in God? Have you ever stopped to think about what that really looks like?

I take refuge in God when I get stressed out. For me, that means going to Bible verses I know bring me comfort. I go to God in prayer. Most of all, I trust in Him no matter what comes my way. That isn't always easy. In fact, sometimes it's downright hard, especially in the midst of heartache. But God is always right there with me. And He's with you, too.

The next time you get overwhelmed or distraught, I hope you'll run to Jesus and rest in His embrace. Let God put a hedge of protection around you. Whether you're anxious or grieving, He can be your refuge.

PRAYER OF GOSPEL GRATITUDE

Father God, thank You for being our refuge in our times of need. I know You are always right there with me and all I have to do is turn into the shadow of Your wings. You are my great God and for that, I am eternally grateful.

12

JESUS LOVES US

May the Lord direct your hearts to the love of God
and to the steadfastness of Christ.

2 Thessalonians 3:5

I was talking to someone on the phone the other day who didn't think God could love her. Have you ever been there? Have you ever wondered how God could love a sinner like you?

The truth is that it doesn't matter who we are or what we've done. It doesn't matter how successful we are, what we look like, or any other condition we can think up. He loves us unconditionally. He loves us because it's who He is (1 John 4:8).

When Jesus was hanging on the cross, He was loving those who put Him there (Luke 23:34). He loved the criminals beside Him (Luke 23:39-43), and He loves us (Romans 5:8).

I take so much comfort in that. When God created us, He created us with a deep-seated need to be loved, a need only He could fill. And He can fill it. When we're alone, He is with us, loving us through it. When we fail, He loves us through it. When we are worn out, He loves us through it.

That's the God we have. And that's something to be thankful for.

PRAYER OF GOSPEL GRATITUDE

Father God, thank You for loving me, even when I don't deserve it, because I can't deserve it. I will never be enough to earn Your love, but You love me anyway. Thank You for that. Help me to remember that Your love is unfailing.

13

JESUS DIED FOR US

God shows his love for us in that
while we were still sinners, Christ died for us.

Romans 5:8

In the beginning, humankind lived in fellowship with God. They walked with Him in the garden of Eden and all of creation lived in harmony.

We shattered our relationship with Jesus when we chose to betray His love for us. We knew what God wanted from us, but we doubted His intentions. The first sin happened there in the garden, but it wasn't the only sin. From that moment, mankind was marked by sin.

Romans 3:23 says, "All have sinned and fall short of the glory of God," but that excludes Jesus. He's the only one who could live a perfect life, because He was both fully man and fully God. That enabled Him to be the perfect sacrifice for our sins.

Romans 6:23 says, "For the wages of sin is death, but the free gift of God is eternal life in Christ Jesus our Lord." That's what I'm thankful for. That Jesus died on the cross for our sins—past, present, and future. Because of Him, we can live a life reunited with God. He restored the fellowship and harmony we gave up back in the garden.

No, life isn't always easy, but we can live knowing we are saved. And that's something to be thankful for.

PRAYER OF GOSPEL GRATITUDE

Father God, thank You for sending Jesus to die on the cross for our sins. Thank You for saving us from ourselves. Lord, there is none like You and I am so grateful for Your love for me.

14

JESUS CONQUERED DEATH

O death, where is your victory?
O death, where is your sting?

1 Corinthians 15:55

Way back in the garden of Eden, God made one rule. "You may surely eat of every tree of the garden, but of the tree of knowledge of good and evil you shall not eat, for in the day that you eat of it you shall surely die" (Genesis 2:16-17).

Yesterday we looked at Romans 6:23 where it says that the wages of sin is death. That's what life has in store for all of us. But when Jesus died on the cross for our sins, He took our punishment upon Himself (Isaiah 53:5).

Yes, we will all still die, but a physical death, not a spiritual one. Jesus died so that we could have everlasting life reunited with the God who created us. That's the heart of today's verse. John 3:16 says it this way, "For God so loved the world, that he gave his only Son, that whoever believes in him should not perish but have eternal life."

Jesus overcame death. Romans 6:9 says, "We know that Christ, being raised from the dead, will never die again; death no longer has dominion over him." And it doesn't have dominion over those who belong to Jesus, either. And that's

us. I don't know about you, but that's something for which I
am eternally grateful.

PRAYER OF GOSPEL GRATITUDE

Father God, thank You for overcoming the spiritual death life
had in store for me. Thank You for loving me enough to die
for me. You didn't have to, but You chose to die for me
because of Your great love. And because You died, You also
rose. You defeated the hold Satan had on me. Thank You.
Help me to live out my love and gratefulness for You today.

15

THE HOLY SPIRIT LIVES IN ME

I will ask the Father, and he will give you another Helper, to
be with you forever, even the Spirit of truth... You know
him, for he dwells with you and will be in you.

John 14:16-17

Jesus is Immanuel, God with us (Matthew 1:23) but it's the
third member of the Trinity that lives inside us. When Jesus
was on earth, He said He was leaving so He could send
another Helper: the Holy Spirit (John 14:26).

The Spirit of God, the Spirit of Jesus, lives inside of every
believer. In Acts 2, Peter said that when we repent and are
baptized, we receive forgiveness for our sins, but we also
receive the gift of the Holy Spirit. And that's what the Holy
Spirit is: a gift.

The Holy Spirit teaches us (John 14:26), intercedes for us
(Romans 8:26), and He gives us hope (Romans 15:13). He fills
us with God's love (Romans 5:5), and so much more. The
Holy Spirit is God within us. He connects us to God in a way
nothing else can. He is our comforter (2 Corinthians 1:3) and
our refuge (Psalm 62:8). Our ever-present help in trouble
(Psalm 46:1). I don't know how I would live life without Him.

That's why today, I'm thankful Jesus sent the Holy Spirit to live inside of me.

PRAYER OF GOSPEL GRATITUDE

Father God, thank You for sending the Holy Spirit to live in me. Thank You that He is with me always. Thank You for the help He gives me when I need it, that He works in my heart always.

16

JESUS GIVES US GRACE

For from his fullness we have all received, grace upon grace.

John 1:16

Do you ever just need a little bit of grace? I know I do. More than a little bit... I need a lot of grace. Thankfully, Jesus gives us grace upon grace (John 1:16).

John 1:14 says, "And the Word became flesh and dwelt among us, and we have seen his glory, glory as of the only Son from the Father, full of grace and truth." Full of grace and truth, that's our Jesus. It doesn't matter who we are or what we've done. Jesus is there for us, giving us grace. We can't out-sin the grace Jesus offers us.

Romans 5 says it this way, "Now the law came in to increase the trespass, but where sin increased, grace abounded all the more, so that, as sin reigned in death, grace also might reign through righteousness leading to eternal life through Jesus Christ our Lord" (vv. 20-21). I love the word picture painted in those verses. Grace abounds.

When I have a rough day and things just don't go my way (by my own fault or otherwise), I know I can turn to Jesus. I know He has the grace I need to keep putting one foot in front of the other, and for that, I am thankful.

PRAYER OF GOSPEL GRATITUDE

Father God, thank You so much for the grace we receive from Jesus. Thank You for His abounding grace. Thank You that I can never use it up or ask too much. Help me to see His grace in my life today. In Jesus's name I pray, amen.

17

WE CAN OVERCOME ANYTHING WITH JESUS

With man this is impossible,
but with God all things are possible.

Matthew 19:26

Romans 12:21 tells us, "Do not be overcome by evil, but overcome evil with good." But that is so much easier said than done. There are so many things I struggle with every day, and I don't always overcome. That's why I'm thankful for Jesus.

I'm thankful for Jesus because even when I don't overcome, I can take heart knowing He has overcome the world (John 16:33). With Christ, I am an overcomer, even when it's hard. Romans 8:37 says, "In all these things we are more than conquerors through him who loved us."

Jesus helps us overcome sin and death, but He's also there to help us through our daily struggles. He can help us overcome anything if we trust Him with it. He gives us hope for a better tomorrow. When we put our trust in Him, we can be overcomers, and that's something I am grateful for.

PRAYER OF GOSPEL GRATITUDE

Father God, thank You for helping me be an overcomer. Thank You for giving me grace when I fail. Thank You for helping me get up, dust myself off, and try again. Thank You for giving me hope.

18

JESUS IS THE CORNERSTONE OF OUR FAITH

For it stands in Scripture:
"Behold, I am laying in Zion a stone,
a cornerstone chosen and precious,
and whoever believes in him will not be put to shame."

1 Peter 2:6

The Christian faith starts and ends with Jesus. The very name *Christian* starts with *Christ*. Jesus is the cornerstone of our faith. Everything else revolves around and builds on Him, and that's a good thing.

We don't have a faith that's too complicated to understand. We don't have to learn 613 commandments to be in with God. We just have to place our faith in Jesus.

We have to trust that God loved us so much He sent His Son to pay the price for our sins. We must believe that Jesus died on the cross for our sins and make Him the Lord of our lives. It's all about Jesus.

Matthew 6:33 says to "seek first the kingdom of God and his righteousness, and all these things will be added to you." When we build our faith on Christ, everything else falls into place. Luke 6 says it this way, "Everyone who comes to me and hears my words and does them, I will show you what he is like: he is like a man building a house, who dug deep and laid the foundation on the rock. And when a flood arose, the stream broke against that house and could not shake it, because it had been well built" (vv. 47-48).

Faith built on Jesus can weather the storms of life. He is our cornerstone and for that, I am thankful.

PRAYER OF GOSPEL GRATITUDE

Father God, thank You for Jesus. Thank You that we can know Him as the cornerstone of our faith, that we don't have to work to build up our faith. Instead, we can put our faith in Him and let everything else fall into place.

19

WE ARE ALIVE IN CHRIST

And you, who were dead in your trespasses and the uncircumcision of your flesh, God made alive together with him, having forgiven us all our trespasses, by canceling the record of debt that stood against us with its legal demands. This he set aside, nailing it to the cross.

Colossians 2:13-14

Romans 6:8 says, "Now if we have died with Christ, we believe that we will also live with him." Because of Jesus, we have died to sin. It has lost its grip on us. And now we can live—really live—with Jesus. Sometimes that looks a lot like it did before we accepted Christ as our Savior, but now we live with hope—hope that this world isn't all there is.

Because of Jesus, we have everlasting life, but everlasting life starts today. When we lean into Jesus, He helps us live a life of love, mercy, grace, and hope for a better tomorrow—hope for eternity with Christ. Mercy, grace, and love for the time between now and then. When we are made alive in Christ, the eyes of our hearts are open, and the whole world looks different.

Today I'm thankful my life isn't what it used to be. I'm thankful I can live with my eyes set on Jesus and full of hope.

PRAYER OF GOSPEL GRATITUDE

Father God, thank You for sending Jesus to die for my sins. Thank You that because of Him I can die to sin, I can die to the old me, and live a new life with Christ in my heart.

20

WE CAN'T LOSE JESUS

For I am sure that neither death nor life,
nor angels nor rulers, nor things present nor things to come,
nor powers, nor height nor depth, nor anything else
in all creation, will be able to separate us from
the love of God in Christ Jesus our Lord.

Romans 8:38-39

I love a certain meme that goes around Facebook every now and then. It has a picture of a door marked with blood to symbolize Passover. It says, "The Lord didn't check who inside the house was worthy. He checked for blood on the doorposts. None of us is worthy. Only the blood of Jesus can cover us." I love the meaning behind it. I love how true it is.

The blood Jesus shed on the cross covers all our sins, all our unworthiness. And it isn't temporary. Once we belong to the family of God, nothing can separate us from it. The blood of Christ can't be washed away. Instead, it washes us, making us white as snow (Isaiah 1:18).

I don't know where today finds you, but I take so much comfort in the fact that we can't lose Jesus. Jesus said, "My sheep hear my voice, and I know them, and they follow me. I give them eternal life, and they will never perish, and no one will snatch them out of my hand" (John 10:27-28). Nothing can separate us from Jesus, and that's something I'm thankful for.

PRAYER OF GOSPEL GRATITUDE

Father God, thank You for Your love for me. Thank You for sending Jesus to the cross to die for my sins. Thank You that His blood is eternal. That it's not something that can be washed away.

21

THE RIGHTEOUSNESS OF CHRIST

For our sake he made him to be sin who knew no sin, so that in him we might become the righteousness of God.

2 Corinthians 5:21

The Bible has so much to say about righteousness, but it all boils down to the fact that, without Jesus, none of us can be righteous on our own. Our righteousness comes from faith in Jesus. Romans 3:10 says, "As it is written: 'None is righteous, no, not one.'" And everyone who believes in Christ is righteous. Romans 3:21-23 says it this way, "But now the righteousness of God has been manifested apart from the law, although the Law and the Prophets bear witness to it—the righteousness of God through faith in Jesus Christ for all who believe. For there is no distinction: for all have sinned and fall short of the glory of God."

We all have the righteousness of Christ credited to us. We can't do it on our own, but through Him we are righteous. That puts a whole new spin on the way we live our lives—with humility. It changes our relationships with others because they also are children of God. It changes everything.

PRAYER OF GOSPEL GRATITUDE

Father God, thank You for crediting me with the righteousness of Christ through faith. Help me remember my righteousness comes from Him, that I can't mess it up, and I don't deserve it, but it's mine, anyway.

22

JESUS IS THE BREAD OF LIFE

I am the bread of life; whoever comes to me shall not
hunger, and whoever believes in me shall never thirst.

John 6:35

I love that the more you dig into God's Word, the more it
seeps into your day. The more you read the Bible, the more
you remember it. Verses will come up when you least expect
them to give you guidance or encouragement, which is why
Matthew 4:4 says, "It is written, 'Man shall not live by bread
alone, but by every word that comes from the mouth of
God.'" Jesus is the Bread of Life, and we need Him in our
day.

When we come to God's Word, it stays with us. Isaiah 55:10-
11 says, "For as the rain and the snow come down from
heaven and do not return there but water the earth, making it
bring forth and sprout, giving seed to the sower and bread to
the eater, so shall my word be that goes out from my mouth;
it shall not return to me empty, but it shall accomplish that
which I purpose, and shall succeed in the thing for which I
sent it." God's Word changes us because Jesus is the very
Word of God. Because He is the Bread of Life, we can let
Him satisfy us.

In Mark 6, Jesus took five loaves of bread and two small fish and fed five thousand men. Jesus, Himself, is like those five loaves of bread. He can feed multitudes, and He is essential to all of us. Just as we could never live without food and water, we can't live without Jesus, our spiritual bread and water.

That's why today, I'm thankful for Jesus, the Bread of Life.

PRAYER OF GOSPEL GRATITUDE

Father God, thank You for Jesus. Thank You for providing spiritual bread for us to consume, but not really consume, Jesus consumes us. He satisfies our souls. Thank You for that.

23

JESUS IS THE LIGHT OF THE WORLD

I am the light of the world. Whoever follows me will not
walk in darkness, but will have the light of life.

John 8:12

John the Baptist came to bear witness to the Light of the
World (John 1:6-8). He came to bear witness about Jesus.
Jesus brought light to the world to give us direction (Psalm
119:105). He is a light to our paths and to our hearts.

But there's more. Because of Christ, we can also share His
light with others. Jesus said of us, "You are the light of the
world. A city set on a hill cannot be hidden. Nor do people
light a lamp and put it under a basket, but on a stand, and it
gives light to all in the house. In the same way, let your light
shine before others, so that they may see your good works
and give glory to your Father who is in heaven" (Matthew
5:14-16). Jesus is a light shining out of us for the whole world
to see.

Jesus is the Light of the World. A light to our paths, a light to
our hearts, and a light for others. That's three things I can be
thankful for.

Father God, thank You for sending Jesus to give light to the world. To say with the psalmist, "For it is you who light my lamp; the LORD my God lightens my darkness" (Psalm 18:28), and I am so glad I'm no longer walking in darkness. Thank You for giving me light.

24

JESUS SHOWS NO PARTIALITY

There is neither Jew nor Greek,
there is neither slave nor free, there is no male and female,
for you are all one in Christ Jesus.

Galatians 3:28

One of my favorite things about Jesus is that He shows no partiality. That means He loves you just as much as He loves me. When the Bible says, "For God so loved the world, that he gave his only Son, that whoever believes in him should not perish but have eternal life," it means that He loved all of us enough to send His Son to die for us—both you and me.

It means that the same gospel that's true for me is true for you, too. It's the same for our pastors, parents, friends, and even our enemies. God loves us all the same, and that's good news. It means every promise in the Bible is true for me (and for you).

It means…

- God will never leave us (Deuteronomy 31:8 and Isaiah 43:2).
- God's grace is sufficient for us (2 Corinthians 12:9-10).

- God can work all things for our good (Romans 8:28).
- God's love for us will never be shaken (Isaiah 54:10).
- We are forgiven (1 John 1:9).
- And so much more.

Because Jesus doesn't have favorites, we can confidently share the gospel with others, knowing it's as true for them as it is for us. And that's something to be thankful for.

PRAYER OF GOSPEL GRATITUDE

Father God, thank You for loving me. But not just me, thank You for loving the world. Thank You for not picking favorites. Help me share Your great love with others.

25

JESUS IS THE WORD OF GOD

In the beginning was the Word, and the Word was with
God, and the Word was God.

John 1:1

Jesus is God's mouthpiece. When God spoke the world into
existence, that was Jesus. When Adam and Eve walked with
God in the cool of the day, that was Jesus. When Moses spoke
to the burning bush—Jesus. Jesus was on Mount Moriah with
Abraham. Jesus is the mediator between God and man (1
Timothy 2:5).

We call the Bible the *Word of God* because that's what it is.
Second Timothy 3:16 tells us that all of Scripture was
breathed out by God. It's got Jesus' fingerprints all over it.
Which is why I'm so thankful for Jesus. We don't just get to
read about Him in God's Word; we get to experience Him.
He speaks to our heart as we read with our eyes.

God's Word is living and active (Hebrews 4:12) just like Jesus,
because it is Jesus. We can have a real relationship with Jesus
through His Word. He can speak into our hearts and lives on
a daily basis. Minute by minute, we can come to Jesus with
whatever is going on in our lives. I'm so thankful we don't

have a God that is silent, but a God who speaks. So today, I'm thankful that Jesus is the Word of God.

PRAYER OF GOSPEL GRATITUDE

Father God, thank You for Jesus. Thank You for the very Word of God that we can read with our eyes and have it speak to our hearts. Thank You for the person of Jesus and the written Word.

26

JESUS GIVES US STRENGTH

I can do all things through him who strengthens me.

Philippians 4:13

Life is hard, but God is good. That's my motto. Part of God's goodness is the strength we get from Jesus, the strength to get through the little things, the big things, and the in-between things. Jesus gives us strength to get through life.

Matthew 6:33 says, "But seek first the kingdom of God and his righteousness, and all these things will be added to you." That's how Jesus gives us strength. When we seek the things of God, Jesus takes care of the rest. Matthew 11:30 says, "My yoke is easy, and my burden is light." Jesus gives us the strength to get through each day, each moment, with Him at our side. Just like when Peter's faith wavered as he walked on water, we can reach for Jesus when we feel like we are going to sink.

We get strength from Jesus by knowing we aren't in this alone. And Jesus said that when we are weak, "My grace is sufficient for you, for my power is made perfect in weakness" (2 Corinthians 12:9). He is our strength when we are weak. That's why I'm thankful for Jesus today.

PRAYER OF GOSPEL GRATITUDE

Father God, thank You for Jesus. Thank You for the strength He gives me to get through each day. Please help me lean into Him when I get run down and weary.

27

JESUS IS FAITHFUL

God is faithful, by whom you were called into the fellowship
of his Son, Jesus Christ our Lord.

1 Corinthians 1:9

The church is often referred to as the *bride of Christ*. We are in
a committed relationship with Jesus, and we couldn't find a
more faithful husband. Deuteronomy 31:8 promises, "It is the
LORD who goes before you. He will be with you; he will not
leave you or forsake you. Do not fear or be dismayed." And
nearly everyone knows Psalm 23, where we find assurance
that God will lead us and walk with us through our darkest
valleys (vv. 2-4).

Another one of my favorite Bible verses is First Thessalonians
5:24. It says, "He who calls you is faithful; he will surely do
it." Whatever Jesus has called us to, we can trust that we don't
have to do it alone. He is faithful to us. Second Timothy 2:13
says, "If we are faithless, he remains faithful—for he cannot
deny himself." Don't you just love that truth?

There are so many promises in God's Word for believers in
Christ, and because Jesus is faithful, we can believe each and
every one of them. He will hear our prayers (1 John 5:14-15).
He will work out everything for our good—even when we

don't see it (Romans 8:28). Moreover, Jesus is faithful to forgive our sins—past, present, and future (Colossians 3:13).

The faithfulness of Jesus penetrates our lives, touching the very recesses of our soul. That's why I'm thankful for Jesus today.

PRAYER OF GOSPEL GRATITUDE

Father God, thank You for the faithfulness of Christ, and that I never have to doubt any of Your promises or face my challenges alone. I am so thankful for Jesus.

28

JESUS INTERCEDES FOR US

For there is one God, and there is one mediator between
God and men, the man Christ Jesus.

1 Timothy 2:5

In the time before Jesus, people had to go through a priest or
prophet to hear from God or to let their requests be made
known. But that's not so anymore. Jesus is our Great High
Priest (Hebrews 4:14) and He intercedes on our behalf. When
He died on the cross, the curtain in the temple was torn in
two. It was designed to separate ordinary people from the
glory of God. But we don't need that anymore because of
Jesus.

Jesus is uniquely qualified to be our mediator because He is
fully man, yet fully God. He walked on the earth, and He
knows what temptation is like. He knows what it is to struggle
(Matthew 8:20). Hebrews 4:15 reminds us, "We do not have
a high priest who is unable to sympathize with our
weaknesses, but one who in every respect has been tempted
as we are, yet without sin." Jesus knows the struggle is real,
and He loves us anyway.

Because of Jesus, the Holy Spirit came to live in our heart and
He knows our prayers before they are even formed on our

lips (Matthew 6:33). When we don't know how to pray, He prays for us (Romans 8:25-27). We don't need a lot of flowery words (Matthew 6:5-7). All we need to do is turn our heart to Jesus. That's why I'm thankful for Jesus today.

PRAYER OF GOSPEL GRATITUDE

Father God, thank You for providing a mediator between us and You. Thank You for bridging the gap that lay between us so You can hear us when we pray.

29

JESUS WILL NEVER LEAVE US

It is the LORD who goes before you. He will be with you; he
will not leave you or forsake you. Do not fear or be
dismayed.

Deuteronomy 31:8

Do you ever feel alone, like you have no friends and no one
you can talk to? I've been there. It's a crummy feeling, but it's
one we can overcome with Jesus.

Jesus promised to be with us always, to the very end of the
age (Matthew 28:20). No matter what we're facing, we can
face it with Jesus in our heart and by our side.

Isaiah 41:10 promises, "Fear not, for I am with you; be not
dismayed, for I am your God; I will strengthen you, I will help
you, I will uphold you with my righteous right hand." Over
and over again, the Bible tells us not to be afraid, because God
is with us, and we can face anything with Jesus.

My soul rests knowing that Jesus will never leave me. No
matter what happens in life, Jesus will always be with me. And
that's why I'm thankful for Jesus today.

PRAYER OF GOSPEL GRATITUDE

Father God, thank You for sending Jesus to be with us always. Thank You that because of Christ, I don't have to face anything alone. Next time I'm feeling lonely, remind me that Jesus is with me always.

30

JESUS IS OUR SAVIOR

And we have seen and testify that the Father has sent his
Son to be the Savior of the world.

1 John 4:14

God created us to love us, but a forced love is no love at all,
so He gave us free will. With that free will, we rejected Him.
He gave us one rule, and we broke it. We chose to listen to
someone other than Jesus.

In the beginning, we chose to reject God's plan for our lives.
We sinned against Him back then, and we continue sinning
against Him today. James 4:17 says, "So whoever knows the
right thing to do and fails to do it, for him it is sin."

Have you ever done the wrong thing? Have you ever known
what was right, but failed to do it? Yeah, me too. Romans 3:23
says, "All have sinned and fall short of the glory of God."
That's bad news, and it gets worse when you read Romans
6:23, "The wages of sin is death."

However, God loves us, so He didn't leave us without hope.
Romans 6:23 also says, "But the free gift of God is eternal life
in Christ Jesus our Lord." That's good news!

We all deserve God's wrath, but instead of condemning the entire human race, God sent His Son to be our Savior. He took the penalty for our sin—all of it. It's all covered by the blood He shed on the cross. And that's why I'm thankful for salvation today.

PRAYER OF GOSPEL GRATITUDE

Father God, thank You for sending Your Son to save us. Thank You for loving me, even though I'm a sinful mess. Please forgive me when I fail You and help me walk in Your ways. In Jesus' name I pray, amen.

25 MORE WAYS
TO BE THANKFUL FOR JESUS

1. Jesus is the way, the truth, and the life.
2. Jesus gave us everlasting life.
3. Jesus is our Defender.
4. Jesus always makes a way.
5. Jesus is the author and perfector of our faith.
6. Jesus has all authority in heaven and on earth.
7. Jesus is the living water.
8. Jesus is our bridegroom.
9. Jesus is our Good Shepherd.
10. Jesus is our High Priest.
11. Jesus is the head of the church.
12. Jesus is the Lamb of God.
13. Jesus is King of Kings and Lord of Lords.
14. Jesus is our Messiah.
15. Jesus gives us hope.
16. Jesus gives us peace.
17. Jesus is our Redeemer.
18. Jesus is our Rock.
19. Jesus is the Son of Man.
20. Jesus is the Resurrection and the Life.
21. Jesus is Lord of all.
22. Jesus is our Wonderful Counselor.
23. Jesus is our Comforter.
24. Jesus is a perfect leader.
25. Jesus is our Healer.

ABOUT HEATHER HART

Heather Hart's first devotional book was published in 2009. The book became an internationally best-selling and award-winning title, and she's been writing ever since. She has written or contributed to over two dozen books, featured articles in the *Christian Women's Voice* magazine, *U Matter Magazine*, online newsletters, as well as countless blogs and websites, including *Candidly Christian* and *Pray with Confidence*.

God has given Heather a heart for ministering to women of all ages and helping them grow in their walk with Him. Her goal isn't to teach women how they can do more, be better, or achieve perfection, it's to point them to Jesus. You can find more of Heather's devotions by visiting *DevotionForToday.com* or visit Heather's online home at *AuthorHeatherHart.com*.

ALSO AVAILABLE

Do you ever feel like the holiday season flies by way too fast?

Heather does. For several years, she woke up on Christmas Eve and didn't even feel like she was mentally ready for Thanksgiving. The holiday season came and went, and she was left feeling like she was grasping at straws. She was so busy trying to do stuff that she wasn't able to enjoy the moments.

One Christmas, Heather was ready to make a change. Christmas was coming, and she wanted her heart to be ready. Join her in this devotional as she builds anticipation for the day we celebrate the birth of our Savior.

Made in the USA
Columbia, SC
28 November 2023

27294681R00043